My First Book About the Five Senses

PATRICIA J. WYNNE
DONALD M. SILVER
ROB DESALLE

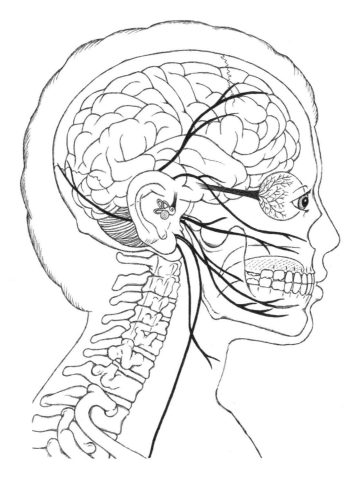

DOVER PUBLICATIONS, INC.
Mineola, New York

For Casper, whose super sense is love.

Your brain uses five senses—seeing, hearing, smelling, tasting, and touching—to figure out what's going on in the world around you. This book explains how your senses work and also gives you detailed illustrations to color. You'll discover similarities and differences between human and animal sensory perception. You'll read about the nervous system, the pathway of sensory information, and how neurons receive and send data. In addition, you will learn how mammals, birds, fish, and other creatures detect heat, use night vision, and find out when it's time to migrate, based on information from their senses.

Bibliographical Note

My First Book About the Five Senses is a new work, first published by Dover Publications, Inc., in 2017.

International Standard Book Number

ISBN-13: 978-0-486-81748-4
ISBN-10: 0-486-81748-2

Manufactured in the United States by LSC Communications
81748201   2017
www.doverpublications.com

WHAT'S GOING ON?
How are the children and the animals using their senses?

1

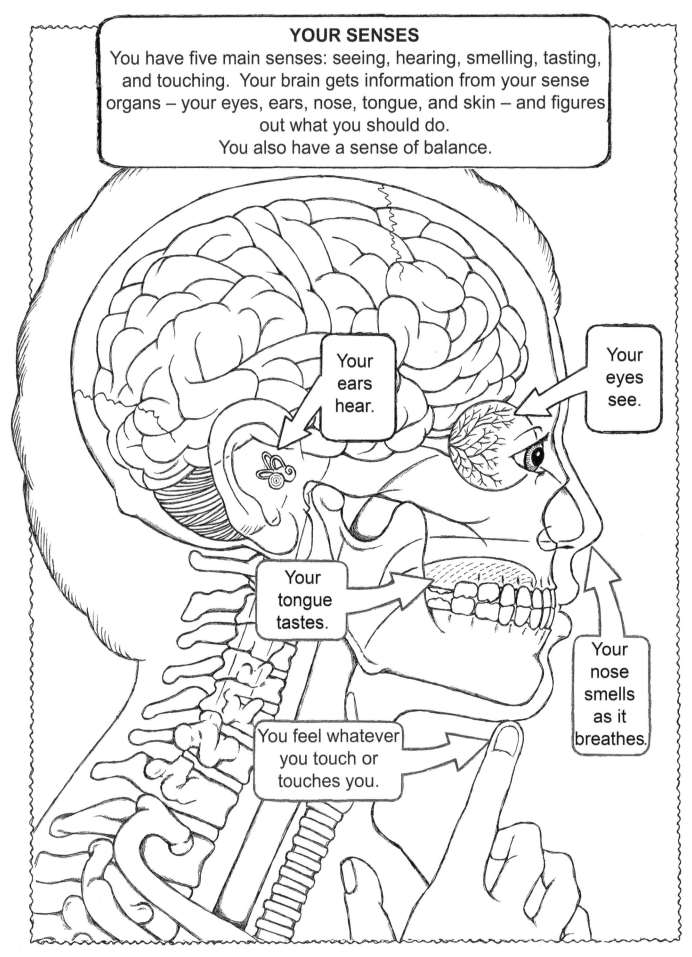

YOUR SENSES
You have five main senses: seeing, hearing, smelling, tasting, and touching. Your brain gets information from your sense organs – your eyes, ears, nose, tongue, and skin – and figures out what you should do.
You also have a sense of balance.

Your ears hear.

Your eyes see.

Your tongue tastes.

Your nose smells as it breathes.

You feel whatever you touch or touches you.

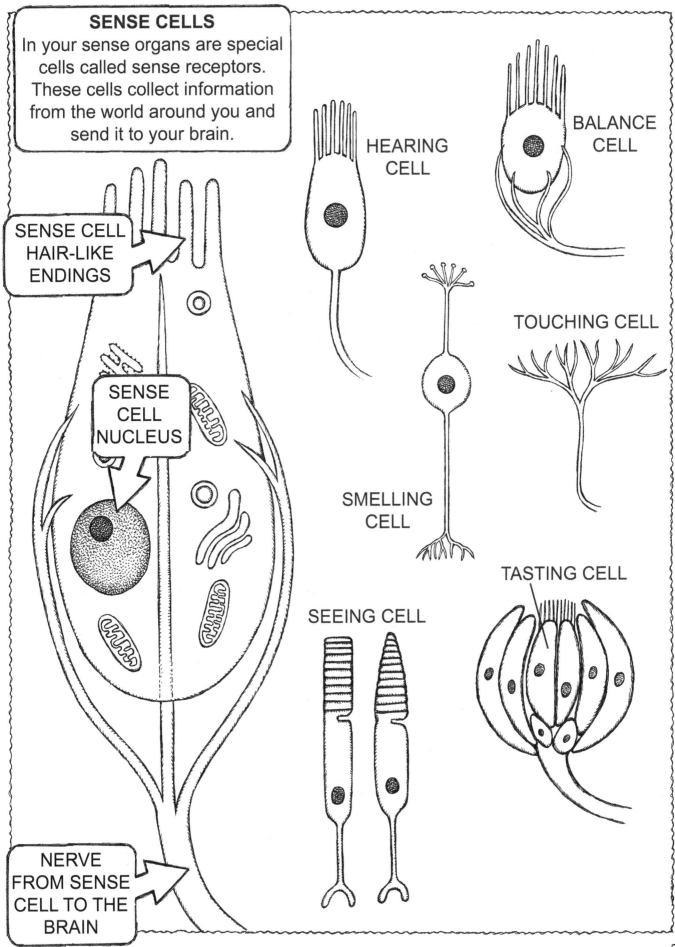

SENSE CELLS
In your sense organs are special cells called sense receptors. These cells collect information from the world around you and send it to your brain.

SENSE CELL HAIR-LIKE ENDINGS

SENSE CELL NUCLEUS

NERVE FROM SENSE CELL TO THE BRAIN

HEARING CELL

BALANCE CELL

TOUCHING CELL

SMELLING CELL

SEEING CELL

TASTING CELL

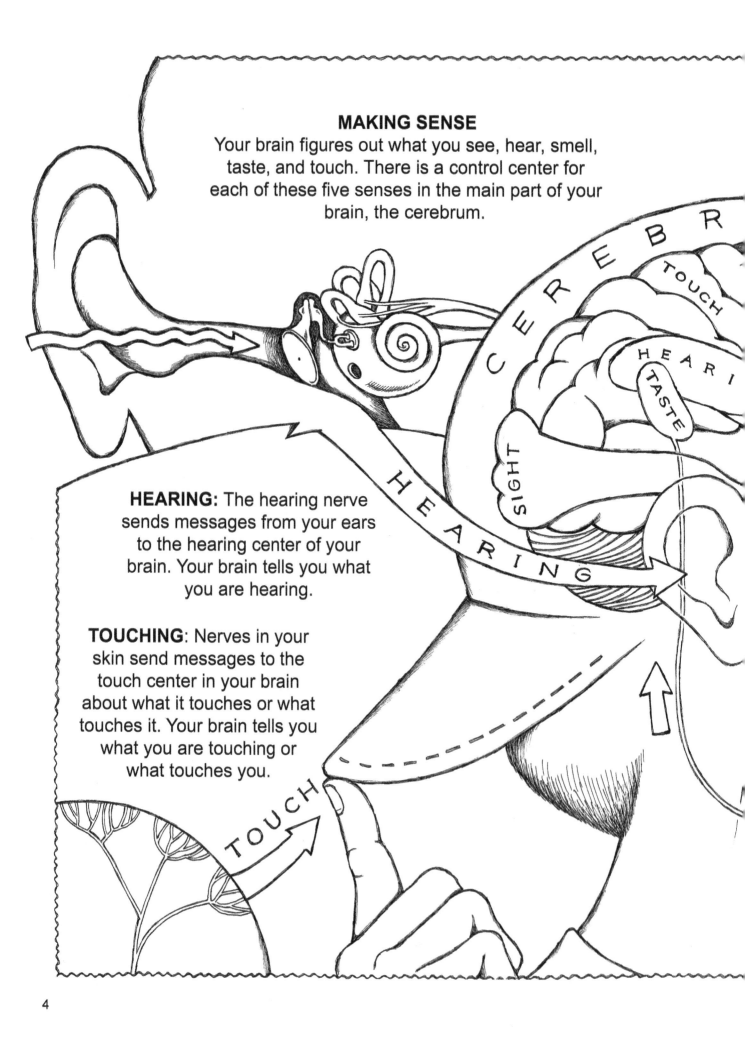

MAKING SENSE
Your brain figures out what you see, hear, smell, taste, and touch. There is a control center for each of these five senses in the main part of your brain, the cerebrum.

HEARING: The hearing nerve sends messages from your ears to the hearing center of your brain. Your brain tells you what you are hearing.

TOUCHING: Nerves in your skin send messages to the touch center in your brain about what it touches or what touches it. Your brain tells you what you are touching or what touches you.

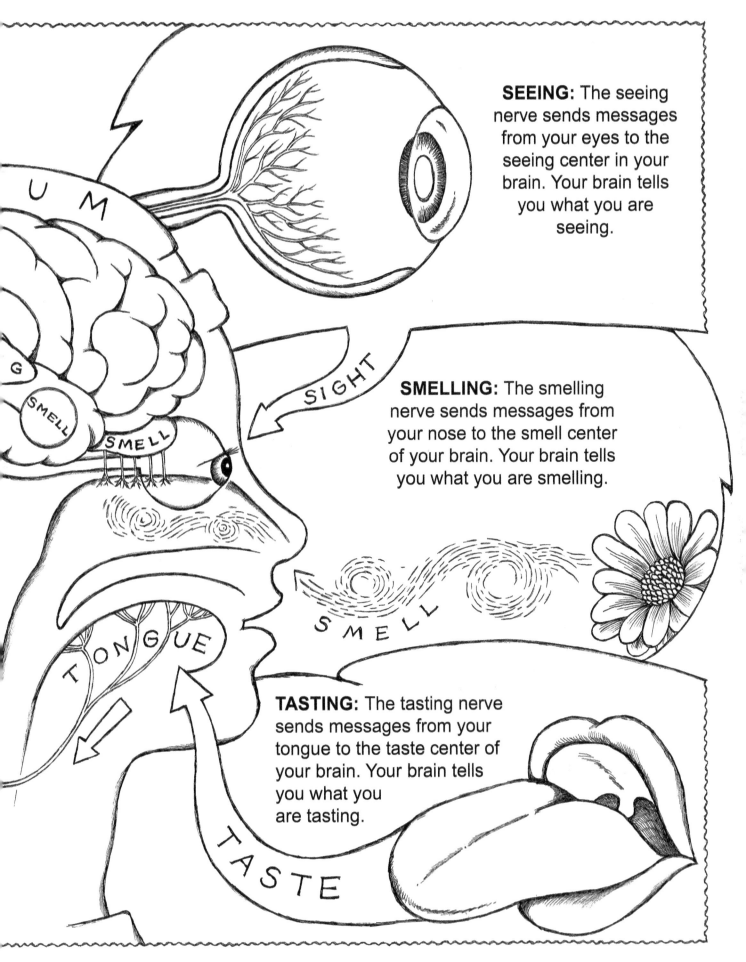

SEEING: The seeing nerve sends messages from your eyes to the seeing center in your brain. Your brain tells you what you are seeing.

SMELLING: The smelling nerve sends messages from your nose to the smell center of your brain. Your brain tells you what you are smelling.

TASTING: The tasting nerve sends messages from your tongue to the taste center of your brain. Your brain tells you what you are tasting.

U M

G

SMELL

SMELL

SIGHT

SMELL

TONGUE

TASTE

5

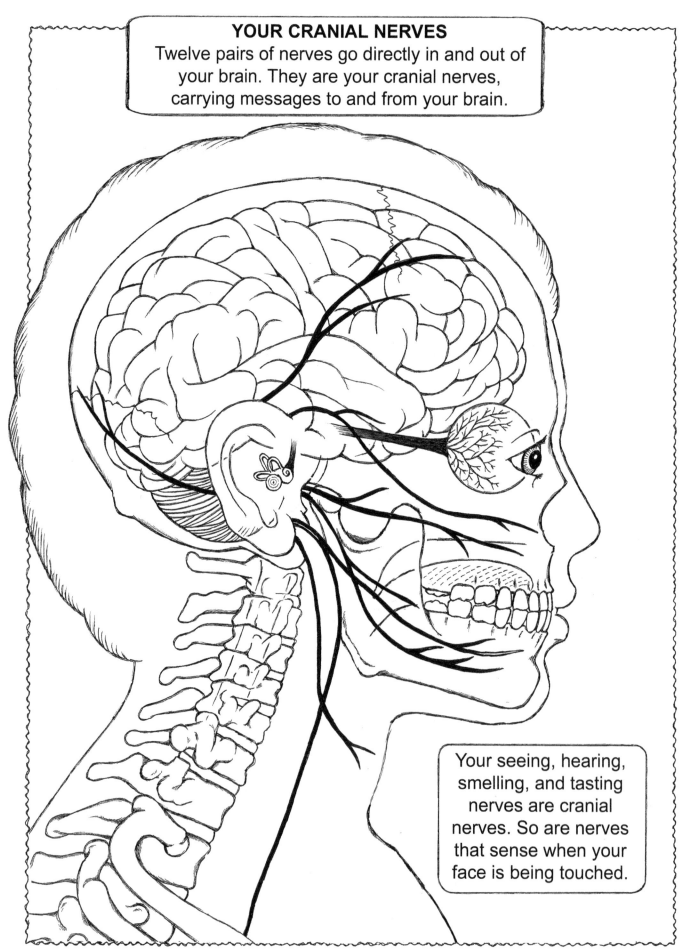

YOUR CRANIAL NERVES
Twelve pairs of nerves go directly in and out of your brain. They are your cranial nerves, carrying messages to and from your brain.

Your seeing, hearing, smelling, and tasting nerves are cranial nerves. So are nerves that sense when your face is being touched.

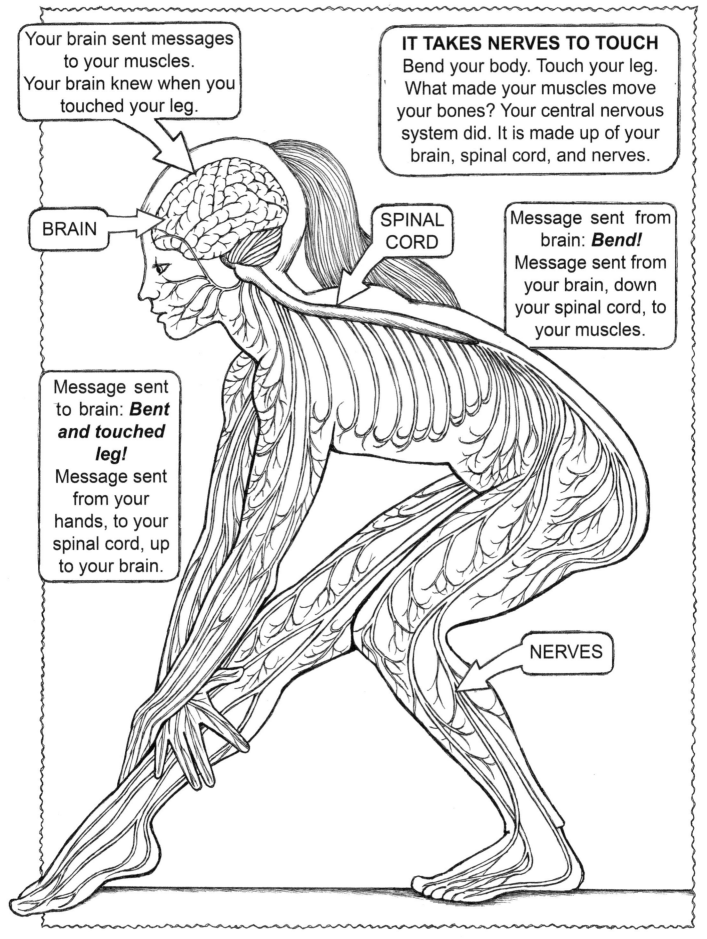

Your brain sent messages to your muscles. Your brain knew when you touched your leg.

BRAIN

IT TAKES NERVES TO TOUCH
Bend your body. Touch your leg. What made your muscles move your bones? Your central nervous system did. It is made up of your brain, spinal cord, and nerves.

SPINAL CORD

Message sent from brain: *Bend!* Message sent from your brain, down your spinal cord, to your muscles.

Message sent to brain: *Bent and touched leg!* Message sent from your hands, to your spinal cord, up to your brain.

NERVES

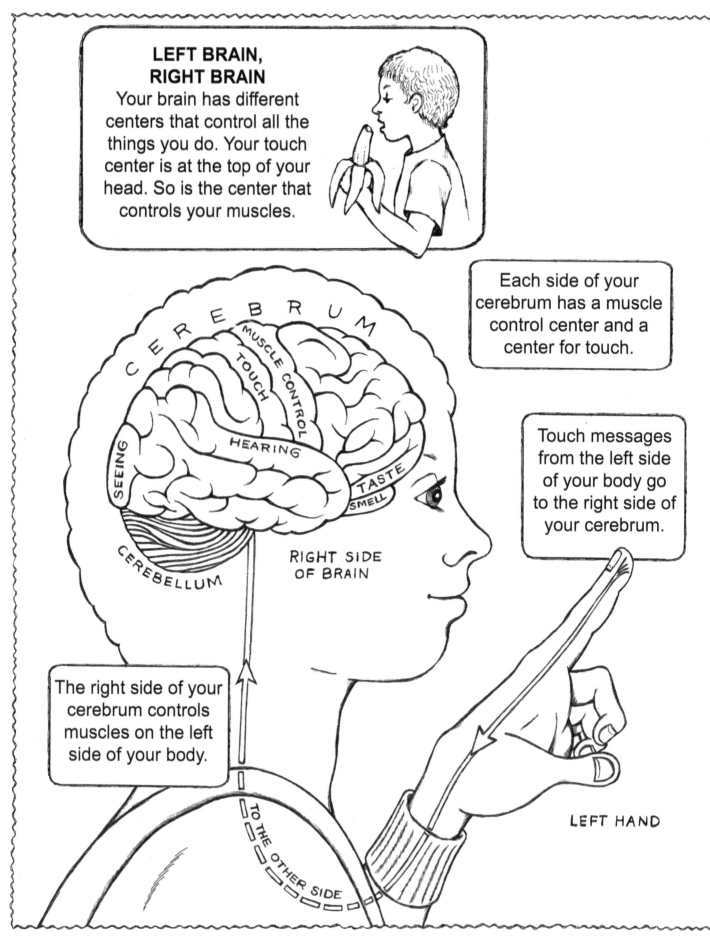

LEFT BRAIN, RIGHT BRAIN

Your brain has different centers that control all the things you do. Your touch center is at the top of your head. So is the center that controls your muscles.

Each side of your cerebrum has a muscle control center and a center for touch.

Touch messages from the left side of your body go to the right side of your cerebrum.

The right side of your cerebrum controls muscles on the left side of your body.

CEREBRUM

MUSCLE CONTROL

TOUCH

HEARING

SEEING

TASTE

SMELL

CEREBELLUM

RIGHT SIDE OF BRAIN

TO THE OTHER SIDE

LEFT HAND

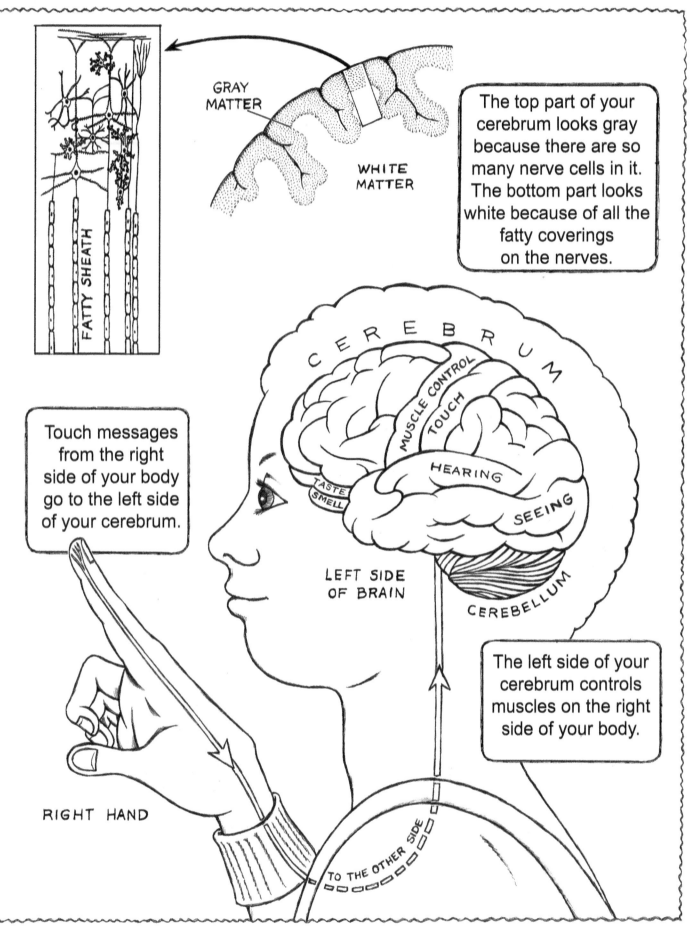

GRAY MATTER

WHITE MATTER

FATTY SHEATH

The top part of your cerebrum looks gray because there are so many nerve cells in it. The bottom part looks white because of all the fatty coverings on the nerves.

CEREBRUM

MUSCLE CONTROL

TOUCH

HEARING

TASTE SMELL

SEEING

LEFT SIDE OF BRAIN

CEREBELLUM

Touch messages from the right side of your body go to the left side of your cerebrum.

The left side of your cerebrum controls muscles on the right side of your body.

RIGHT HAND

TO THE OTHER SIDE

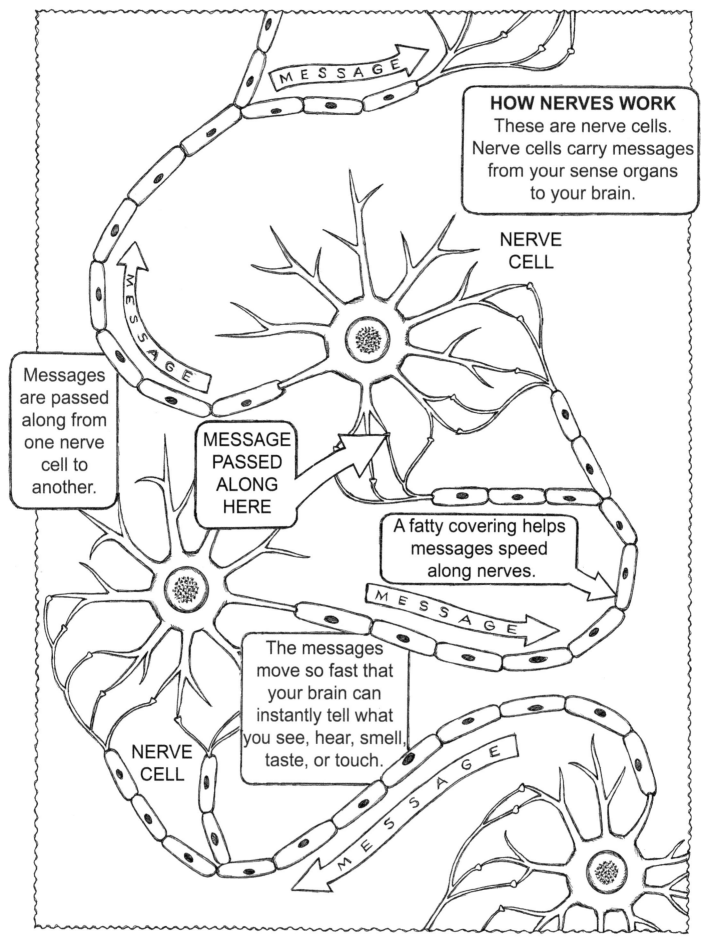

10

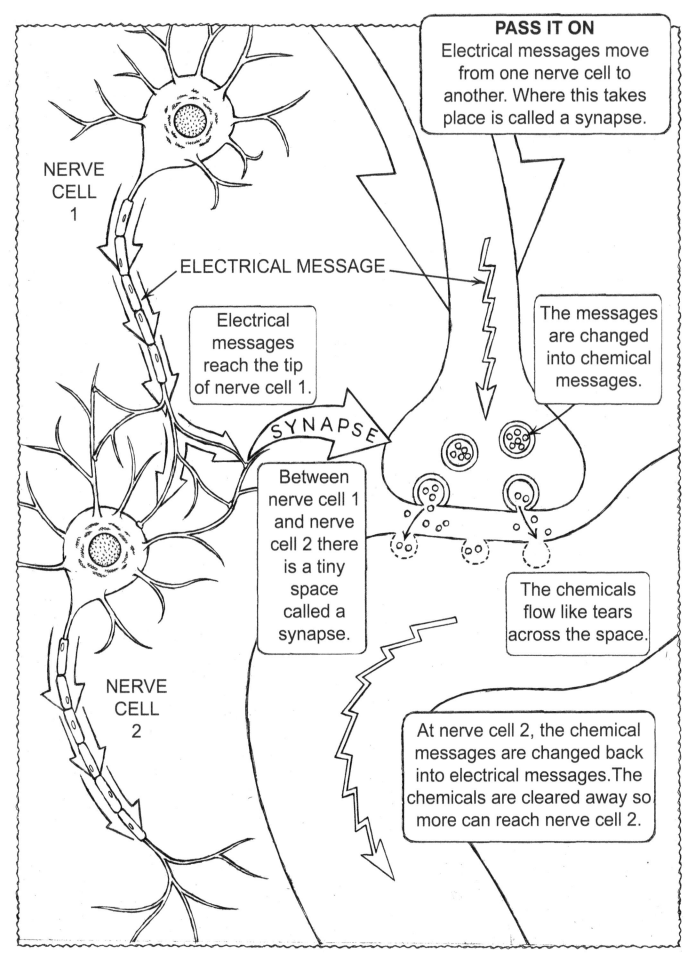

11

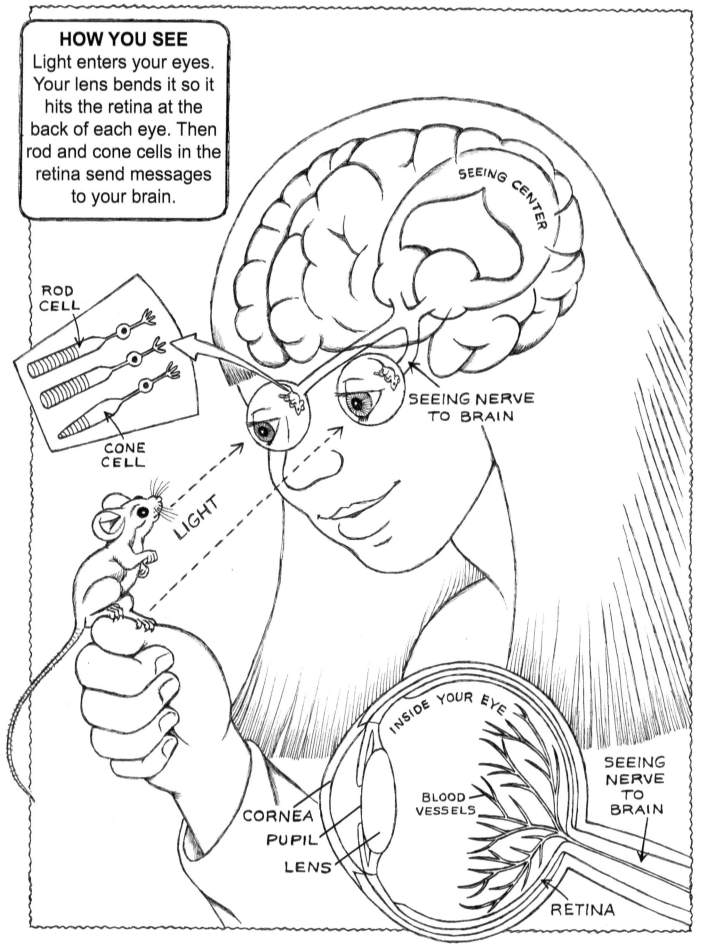

HOW YOU SEE
Light enters your eyes. Your lens bends it so it hits the retina at the back of each eye. Then rod and cone cells in the retina send messages to your brain.

SEEING CENTER

ROD CELL

CONE CELL

SEEING NERVE TO BRAIN

LIGHT

INSIDE YOUR EYE

BLOOD VESSELS

SEEING NERVE TO BRAIN

CORNEA
PUPIL
LENS

RETINA

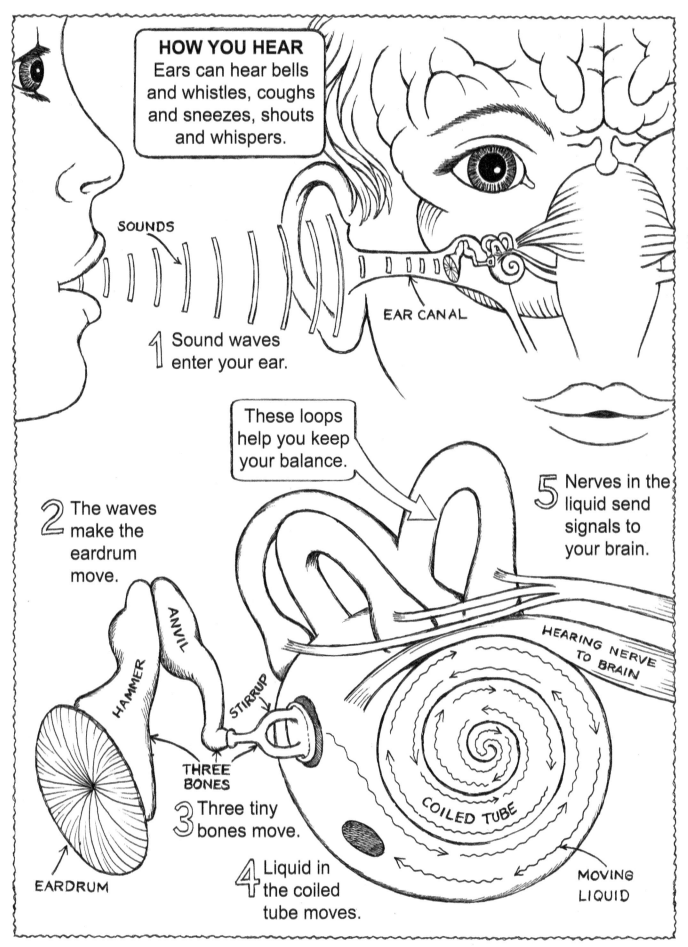

HOW YOU HEAR
Ears can hear bells and whistles, coughs and sneezes, shouts and whispers.

SOUNDS

EAR CANAL

1 Sound waves enter your ear.

These loops help you keep your balance.

2 The waves make the eardrum move.

5 Nerves in the liquid send signals to your brain.

ANVIL

HAMMER

STIRRUP

HEARING NERVE TO BRAIN

THREE BONES

3 Three tiny bones move.

EARDRUM

COILED TUBE

4 Liquid in the coiled tube moves.

MOVING LIQUID

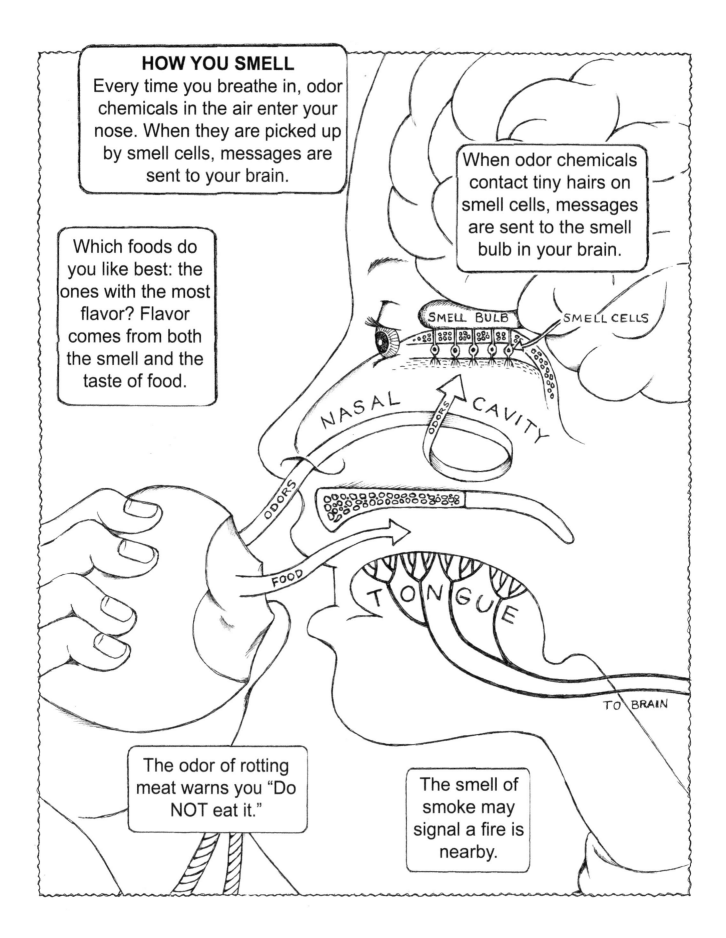

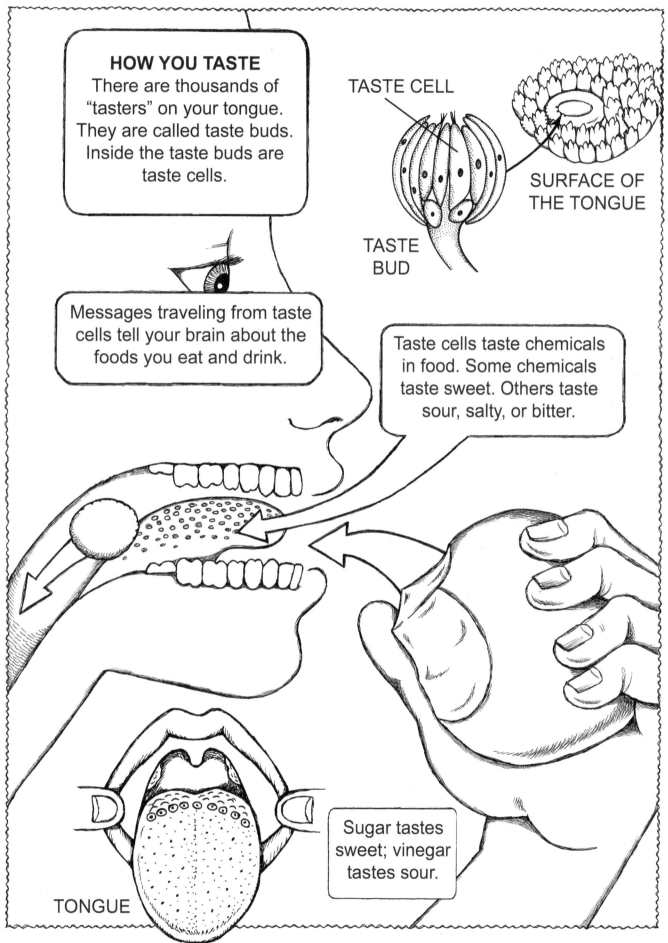

HOW YOU TASTE
There are thousands of "tasters" on your tongue. They are called taste buds. Inside the taste buds are taste cells.

TASTE CELL

SURFACE OF THE TONGUE

TASTE BUD

Messages traveling from taste cells tell your brain about the foods you eat and drink.

Taste cells taste chemicals in food. Some chemicals taste sweet. Others taste sour, salty, or bitter.

Sugar tastes sweet; vinegar tastes sour.

TONGUE

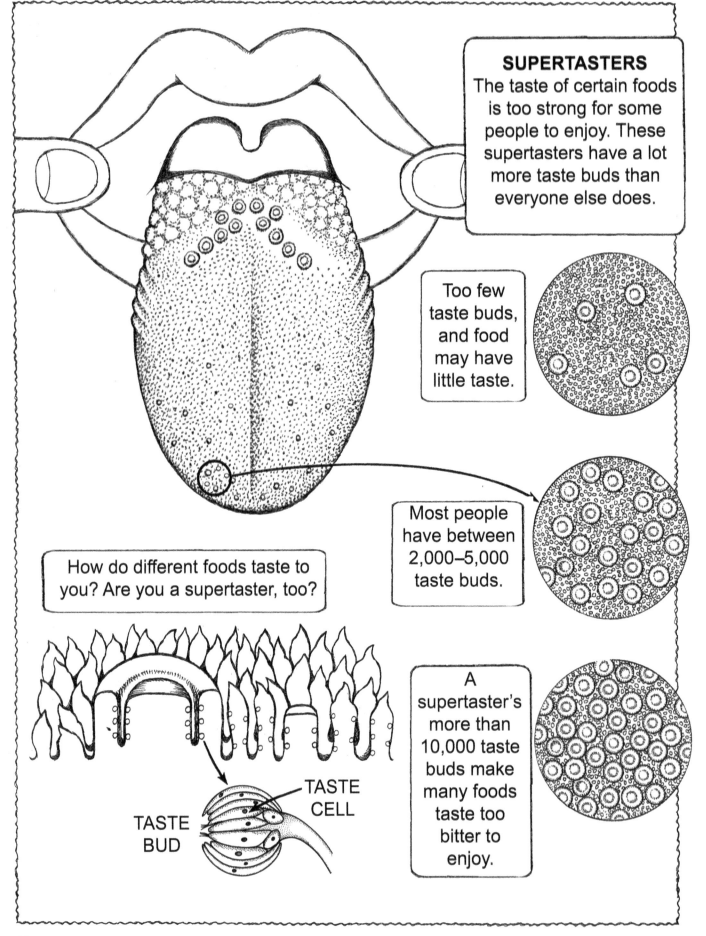

SUPERTASTERS
The taste of certain foods is too strong for some people to enjoy. These supertasters have a lot more taste buds than everyone else does.

Too few taste buds, and food may have little taste.

How do different foods taste to you? Are you a supertaster, too?

Most people have between 2,000–5,000 taste buds.

A supertaster's more than 10,000 taste buds make many foods taste too bitter to enjoy.

TASTE CELL

TASTE BUD

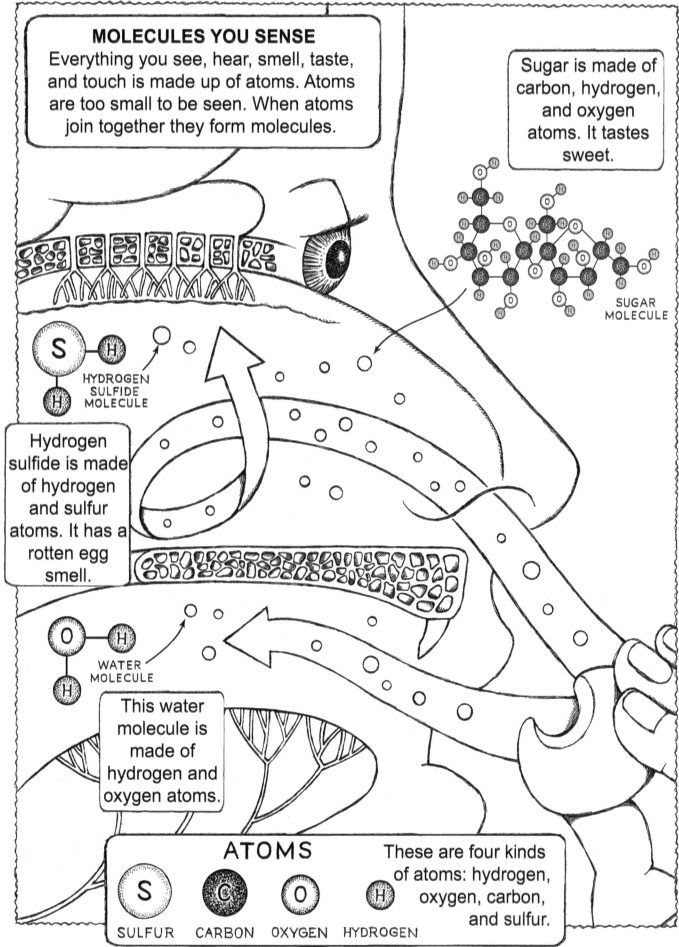

MOLECULES YOU SENSE
Everything you see, hear, smell, taste, and touch is made up of atoms. Atoms are too small to be seen. When atoms join together they form molecules.

Sugar is made of carbon, hydrogen, and oxygen atoms. It tastes sweet.

SUGAR MOLECULE

HYDROGEN SULFIDE MOLECULE

Hydrogen sulfide is made of hydrogen and sulfur atoms. It has a rotten egg smell.

WATER MOLECULE

This water molecule is made of hydrogen and oxygen atoms.

ATOMS

SULFUR CARBON OXYGEN HYDROGEN

These are four kinds of atoms: hydrogen, oxygen, carbon, and sulfur.

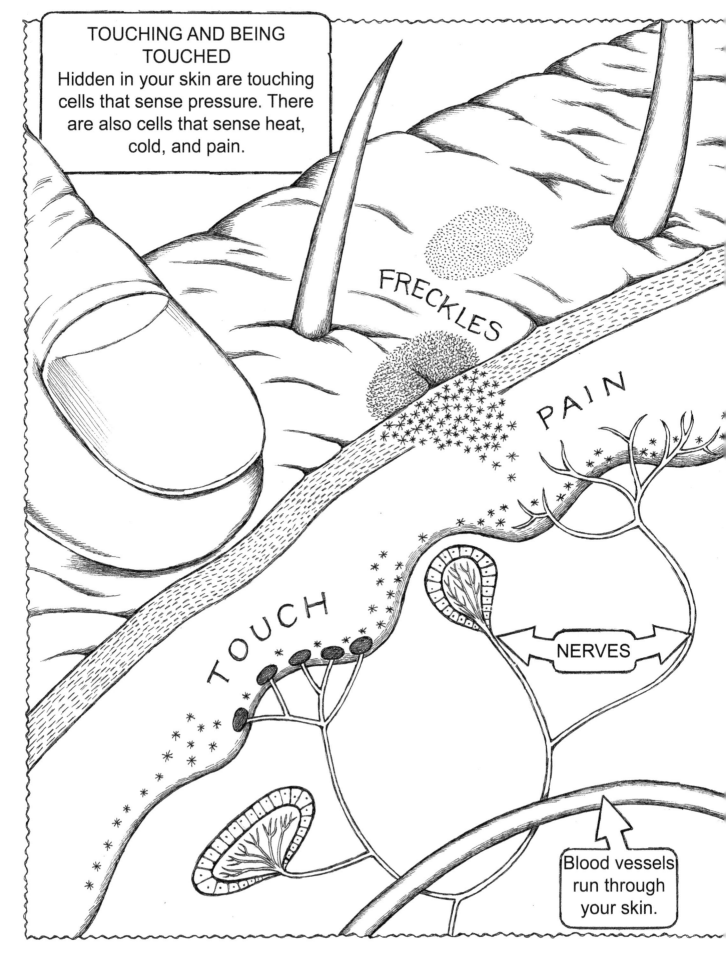

TOUCHING AND BEING TOUCHED
Hidden in your skin are touching cells that sense pressure. There are also cells that sense heat, cold, and pain.

FRECKLES

PAIN

TOUCH

NERVES

Blood vessels run through your skin.

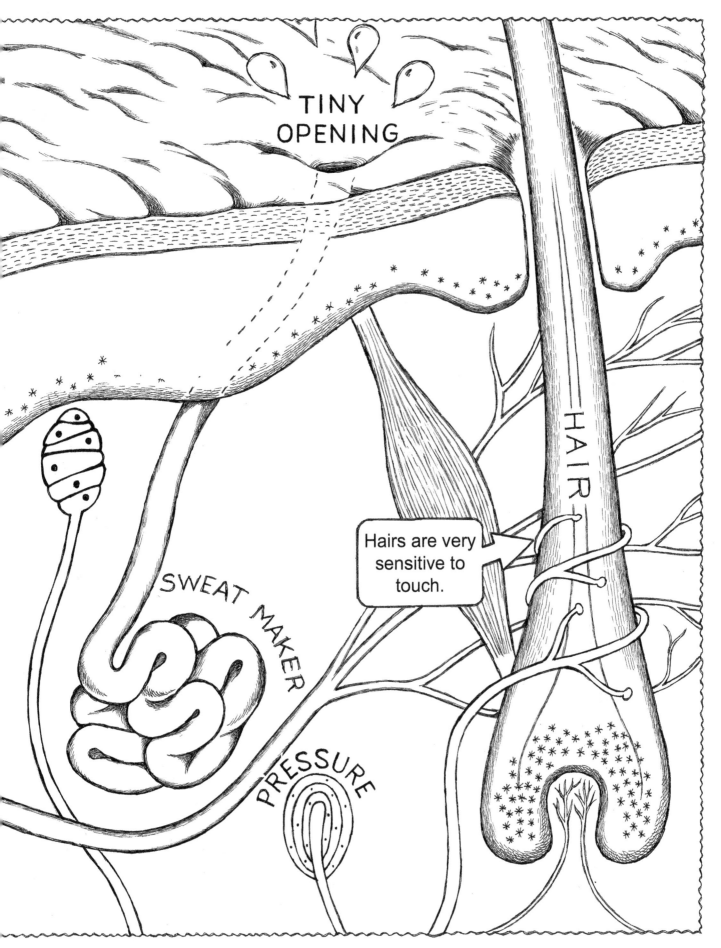

KEEPING YOUR BALANCE
Three loops inside each ear send messages to your cerebellum to help keep you balanced.

When you spin around and stop suddenly, the fluid in the three loops keeps moving. This confuses your brain. It thinks you are still moving, and that makes you feel dizzy.

When you move your head, the fluid in each loop moves, too. When nerves sense the movement, your brain can figure out where your head is.

YOUR "LITTLE BRAIN"
Your cerebellum helps you stay balanced. It receives messages from the loops in your ears and relays them to your cerebrum to help your muscles work together.

CEREBRUM

BRAIN STEM

CEREBELLUM

The word cerebellum means "little brain."

CEREBELLUM

Inside each loop are balance hair cells and fluid that move when your head does. Without staying balanced, you could not run, jump, dance, or skateboard.

BALANCE HAIR CELLS

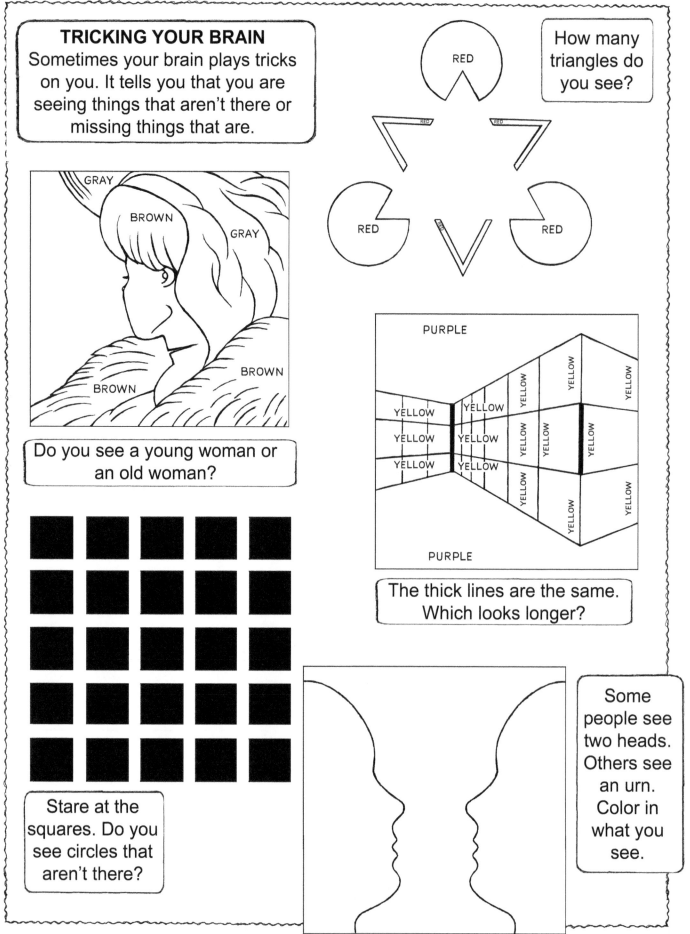

TRICKING YOUR BRAIN
Sometimes your brain plays tricks on you. It tells you that you are seeing things that aren't there or missing things that are.

How many triangles do you see?

GRAY
BROWN
GRAY
BROWN
BROWN

Do you see a young woman or an old woman?

RED
RED
RED
RED
RED

PURPLE
YELLOW
YELLOW
YELLOW
YELLOW
YELLOW
YELLOW
YELLOW
YELLOW
YELLOW
YELLOW
YELLOW
YELLOW
YELLOW
YELLOW
PURPLE

The thick lines are the same. Which looks longer?

Stare at the squares. Do you see circles that aren't there?

Some people see two heads. Others see an urn. Color in what you see.

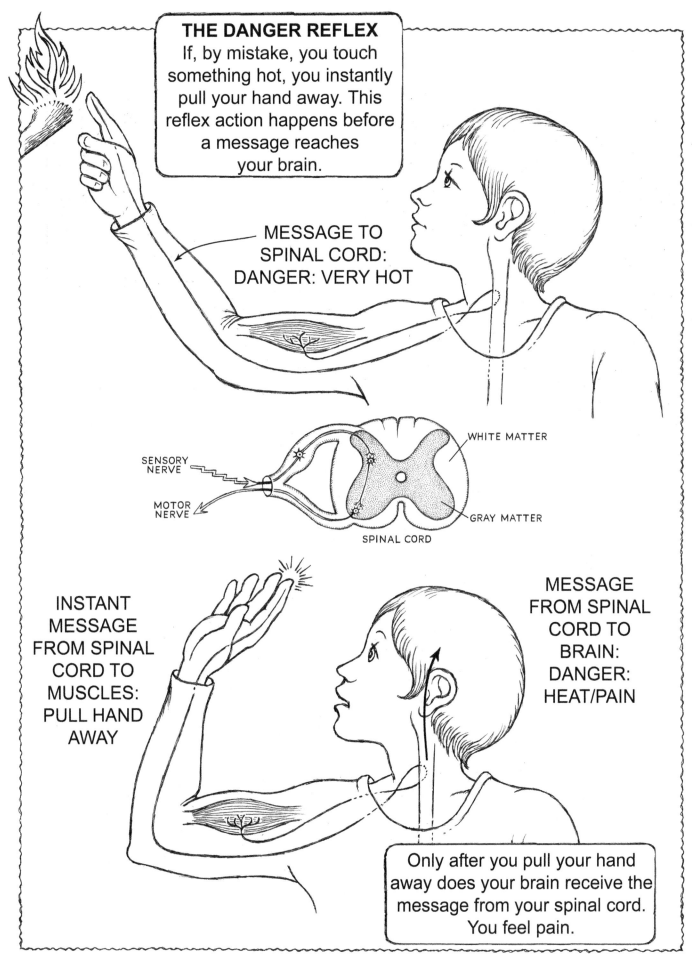

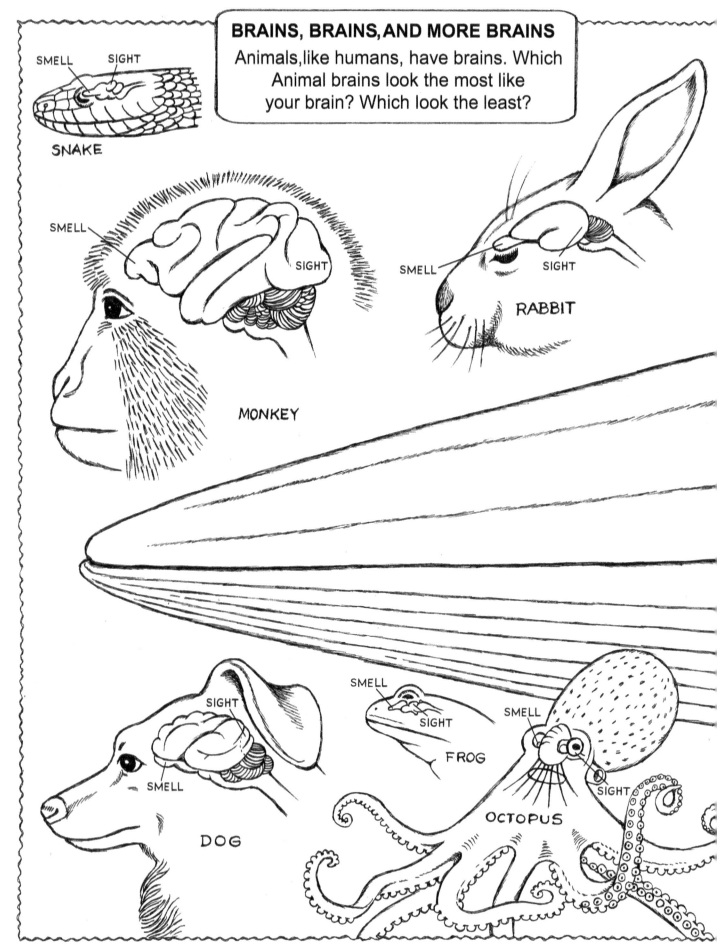

SMELL SIGHT

SNAKE

BRAINS, BRAINS, AND MORE BRAINS
Animals, like humans, have brains. Which
Animal brains look the most like
your brain? Which look the least?

SMELL

SIGHT

MONKEY

SMELL SIGHT

RABBIT

SIGHT

SMELL

DOG

SMELL

SIGHT

FROG

SMELL

SIGHT

OCTOPUS

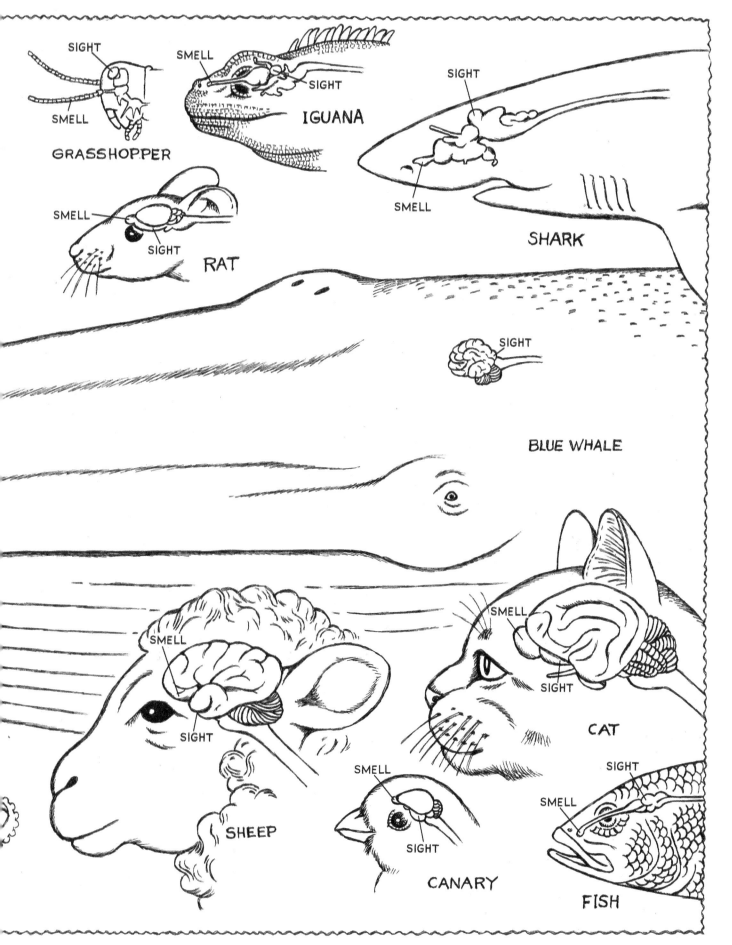

SIGHT

SMELL

SMELL

GRASSHOPPER

SMELL

SIGHT

IGUANA

SIGHT

SMELL

SHARK

SMELL

SIGHT

RAT

SIGHT

BLUE WHALE

SMELL

SIGHT

SHEEP

SMELL

SIGHT

CAT

SMELL

SIGHT

CANARY

SIGHT

SMELL

FISH

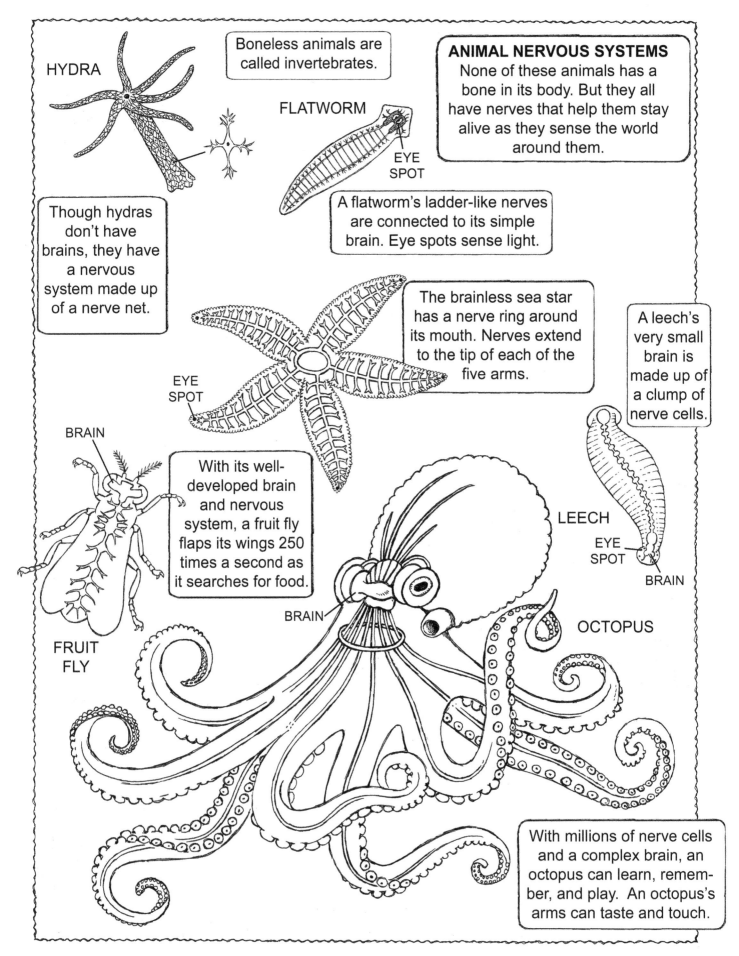

HYDRA

Boneless animals are called invertebrates.

FLATWORM

EYE SPOT

ANIMAL NERVOUS SYSTEMS
None of these animals has a bone in its body. But they all have nerves that help them stay alive as they sense the world around them.

A flatworm's ladder-like nerves are connected to its simple brain. Eye spots sense light.

Though hydras don't have brains, they have a nervous system made up of a nerve net.

The brainless sea star has a nerve ring around its mouth. Nerves extend to the tip of each of the five arms.

A leech's very small brain is made up of a clump of nerve cells.

EYE SPOT

BRAIN

With its well-developed brain and nervous system, a fruit fly flaps its wings 250 times a second as it searches for food.

LEECH

EYE SPOT

BRAIN

BRAIN

OCTOPUS

FRUIT FLY

With millions of nerve cells and a complex brain, an octopus can learn, remember, and play. An octopus's arms can taste and touch.

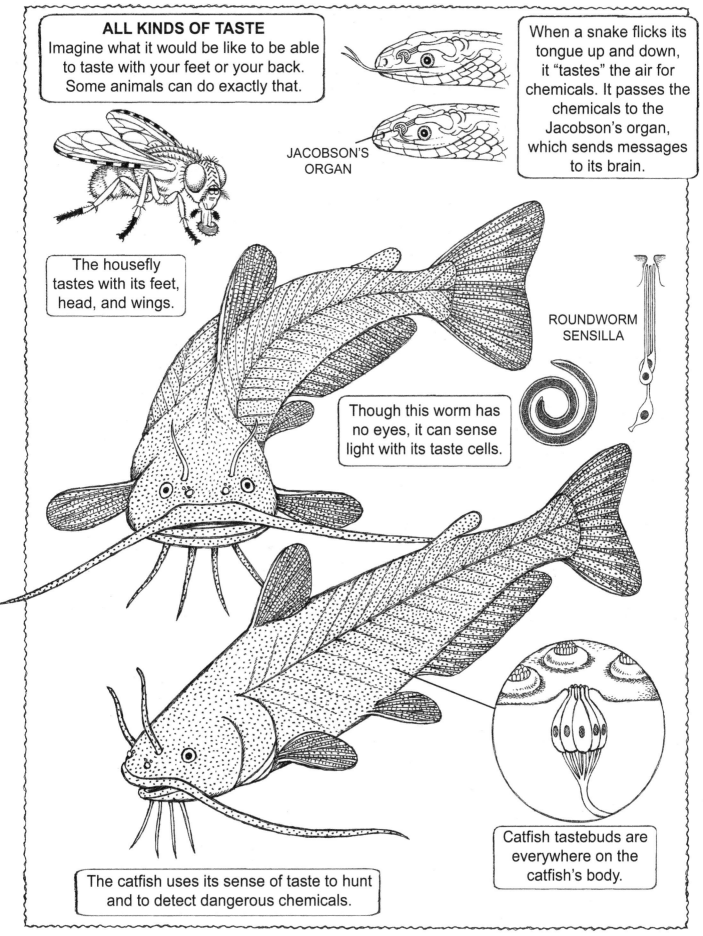

ALL KINDS OF TASTE
Imagine what it would be like to be able to taste with your feet or your back. Some animals can do exactly that.

When a snake flicks its tongue up and down, it "tastes" the air for chemicals. It passes the chemicals to the Jacobson's organ, which sends messages to its brain.

JACOBSON'S ORGAN

The housefly tastes with its feet, head, and wings.

ROUNDWORM SENSILLA

Though this worm has no eyes, it can sense light with its taste cells.

Catfish tastebuds are everywhere on the catfish's body.

The catfish uses its sense of taste to hunt and to detect dangerous chemicals.

27

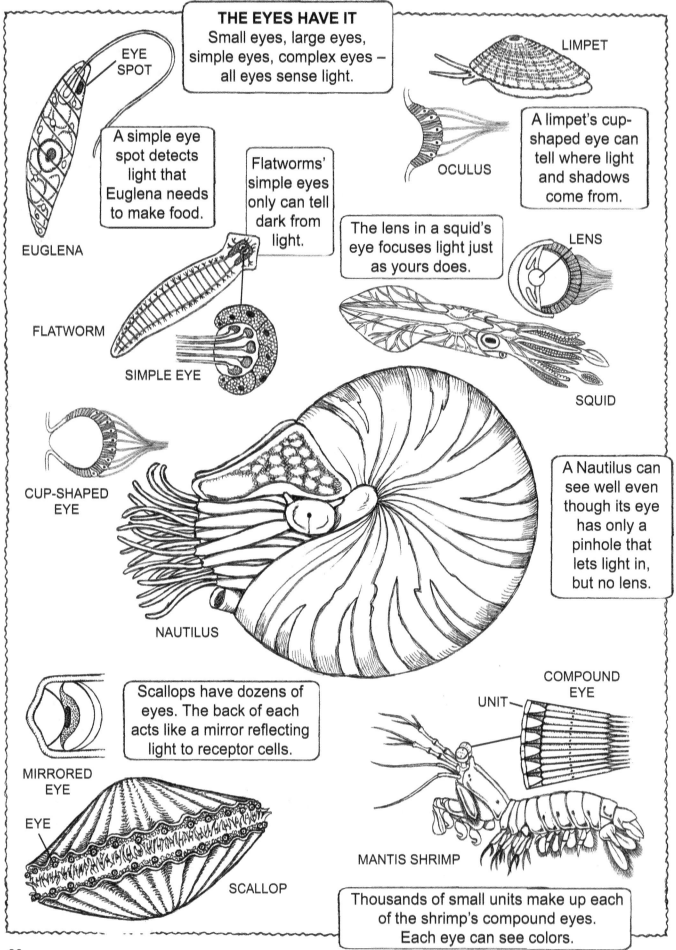

THE EYES HAVE IT
Small eyes, large eyes,
simple eyes, complex eyes –
all eyes sense light.

EYE SPOT

LIMPET

A simple eye spot detects light that Euglena needs to make food.

EUGLENA

Flatworms' simple eyes only can tell dark from light.

OCULUS

A limpet's cup-shaped eye can tell where light and shadows come from.

The lens in a squid's eye focuses light just as yours does.

LENS

FLATWORM

SIMPLE EYE

SQUID

CUP-SHAPED EYE

A Nautilus can see well even though its eye has only a pinhole that lets light in, but no lens.

NAUTILUS

COMPOUND EYE

UNIT

Scallops have dozens of eyes. The back of each acts like a mirror reflecting light to receptor cells.

MIRRORED EYE

EYE

MANTIS SHRIMP

SCALLOP

Thousands of small units make up each of the shrimp's compound eyes. Each eye can see colors.

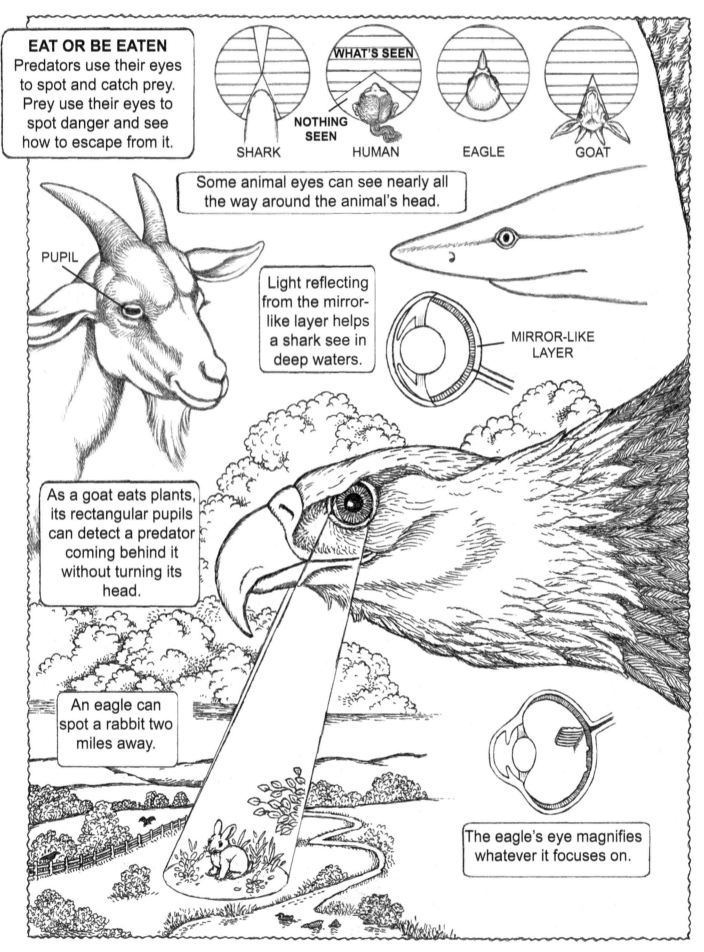

EAT OR BE EATEN
Predators use their eyes to spot and catch prey. Prey use their eyes to spot danger and see how to escape from it.

WHAT'S SEEN

NOTHING SEEN

SHARK HUMAN EAGLE GOAT

Some animal eyes can see nearly all the way around the animal's head.

PUPIL

Light reflecting from the mirror-like layer helps a shark see in deep waters.

MIRROR-LIKE LAYER

As a goat eats plants, its rectangular pupils can detect a predator coming behind it without turning its head.

An eagle can spot a rabbit two miles away.

The eagle's eye magnifies whatever it focuses on.

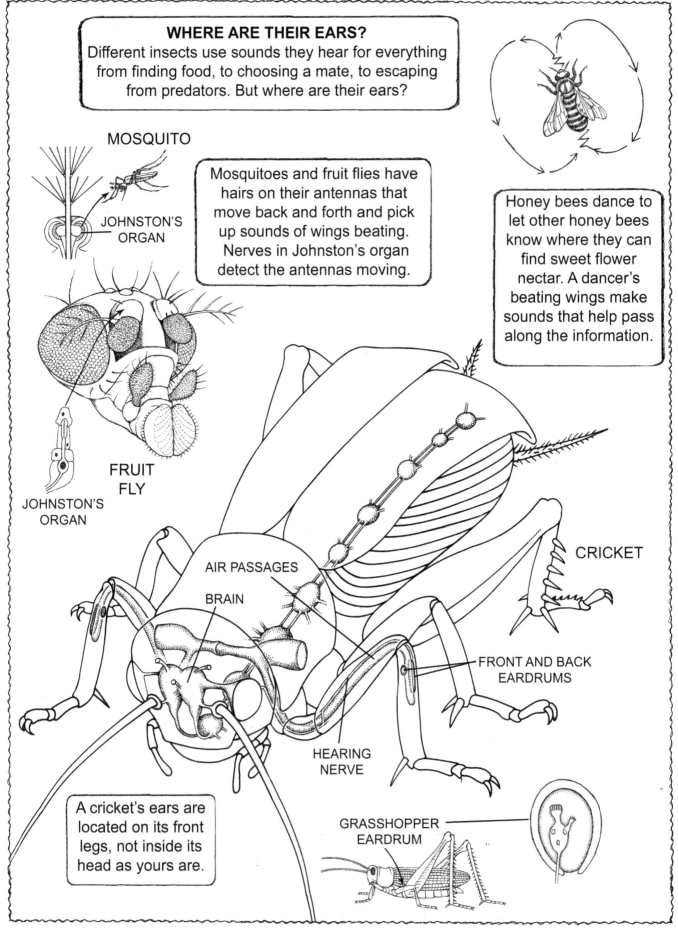

WHERE ARE THEIR EARS?
Different insects use sounds they hear for everything from finding food, to choosing a mate, to escaping from predators. But where are their ears?

MOSQUITO

JOHNSTON'S ORGAN

Mosquitoes and fruit flies have hairs on their antennas that move back and forth and pick up sounds of wings beating. Nerves in Johnston's organ detect the antennas moving.

Honey bees dance to let other honey bees know where they can find sweet flower nectar. A dancer's beating wings make sounds that help pass along the information.

FRUIT FLY

JOHNSTON'S ORGAN

CRICKET

AIR PASSAGES

BRAIN

FRONT AND BACK EARDRUMS

HEARING NERVE

A cricket's ears are located on its front legs, not inside its head as yours are.

GRASSHOPPER EARDRUM

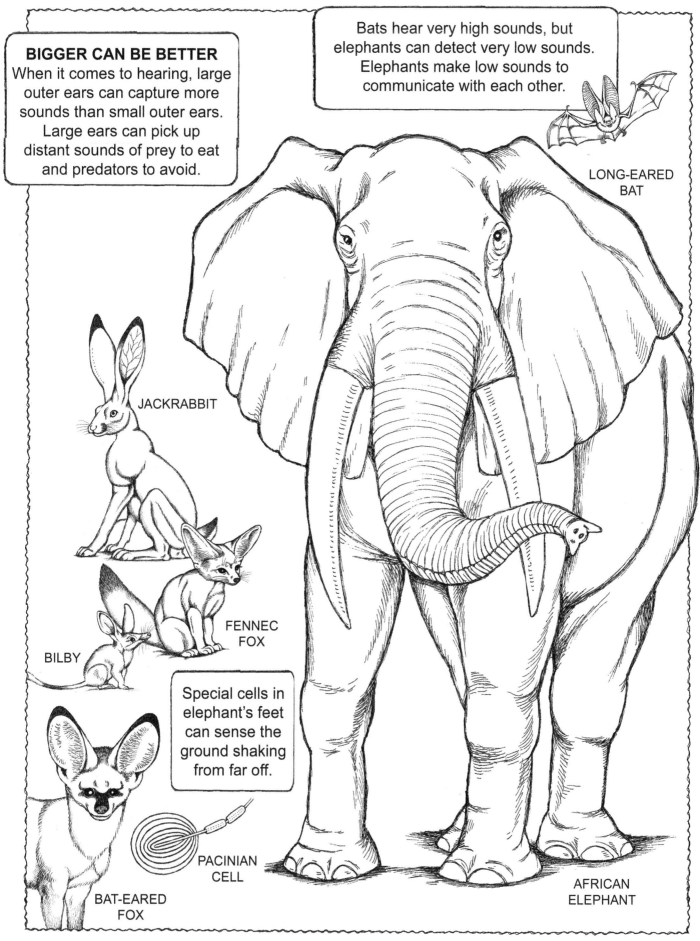

BIGGER CAN BE BETTER
When it comes to hearing, large outer ears can capture more sounds than small outer ears. Large ears can pick up distant sounds of prey to eat and predators to avoid.

Bats hear very high sounds, but elephants can detect very low sounds. Elephants make low sounds to communicate with each other.

LONG-EARED BAT

JACKRABBIT

FENNEC FOX

BILBY

Special cells in elephant's feet can sense the ground shaking from far off.

PACINIAN CELL

BAT-EARED FOX

AFRICAN ELEPHANT

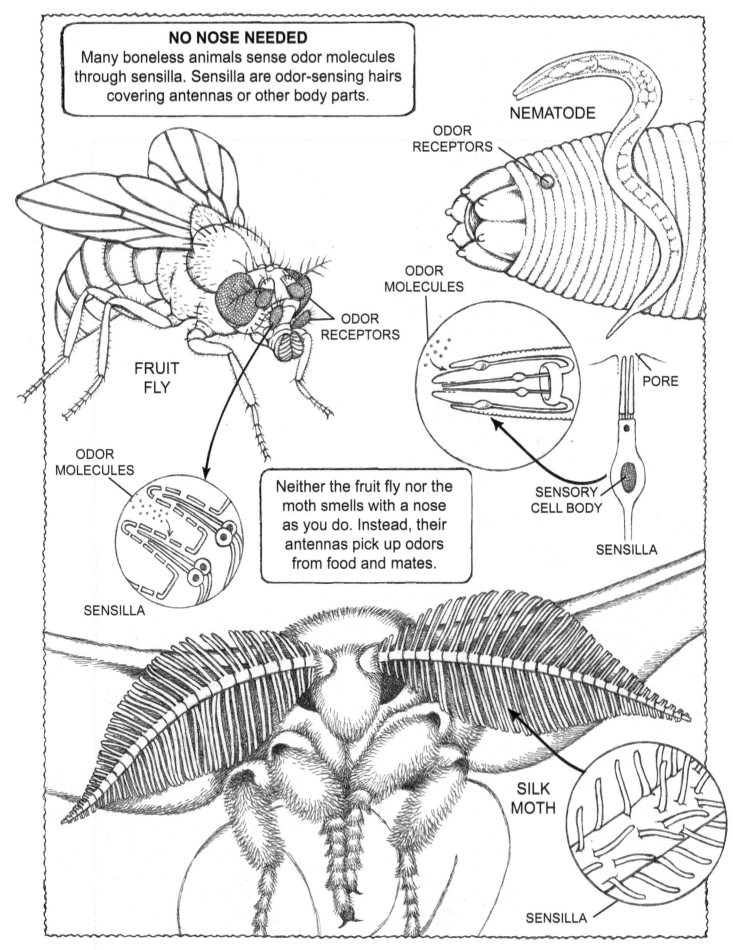

NO NOSE NEEDED

Many boneless animals sense odor molecules through sensilla. Sensilla are odor-sensing hairs covering antennas or other body parts.

NEMATODE

ODOR RECEPTORS

ODOR MOLECULES

PORE

SENSORY CELL BODY

SENSILLA

ODOR RECEPTORS

FRUIT FLY

ODOR MOLECULES

Neither the fruit fly nor the moth smells with a nose as you do. Instead, their antennas pick up odors from food and mates.

SENSILLA

SILK MOTH

SENSILLA

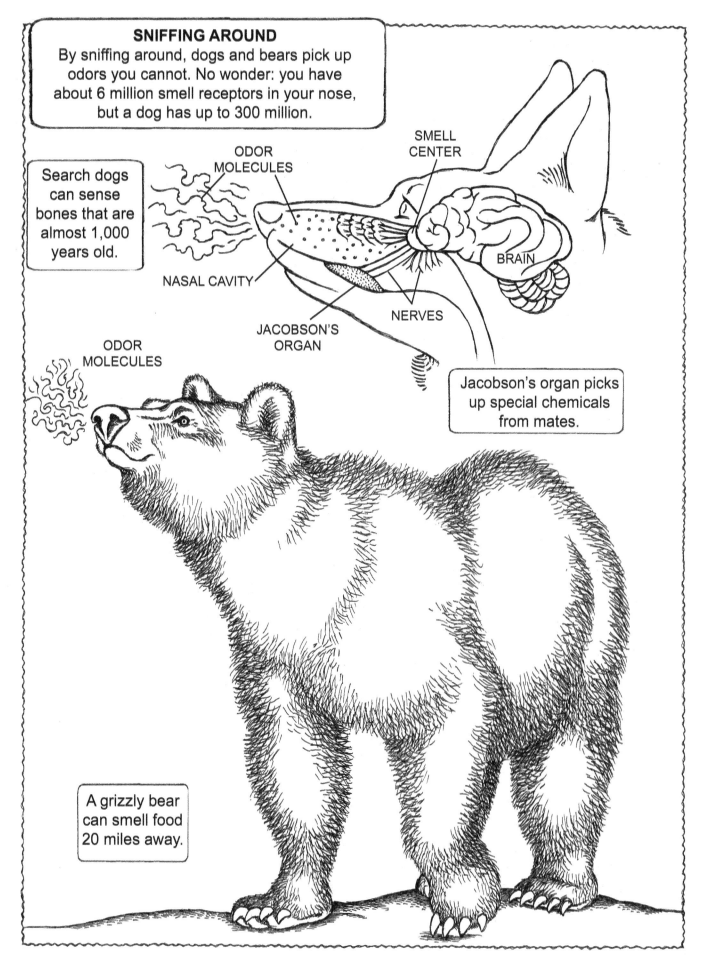

SNIFFING AROUND
By sniffing around, dogs and bears pick up odors you cannot. No wonder: you have about 6 million smell receptors in your nose, but a dog has up to 300 million.

ODOR MOLECULES

SMELL CENTER

Search dogs can sense bones that are almost 1,000 years old.

NASAL CAVITY

JACOBSON'S ORGAN

NERVES

BRAIN

Jacobson's organ picks up special chemicals from mates.

ODOR MOLECULES

A grizzly bear can smell food 20 miles away.

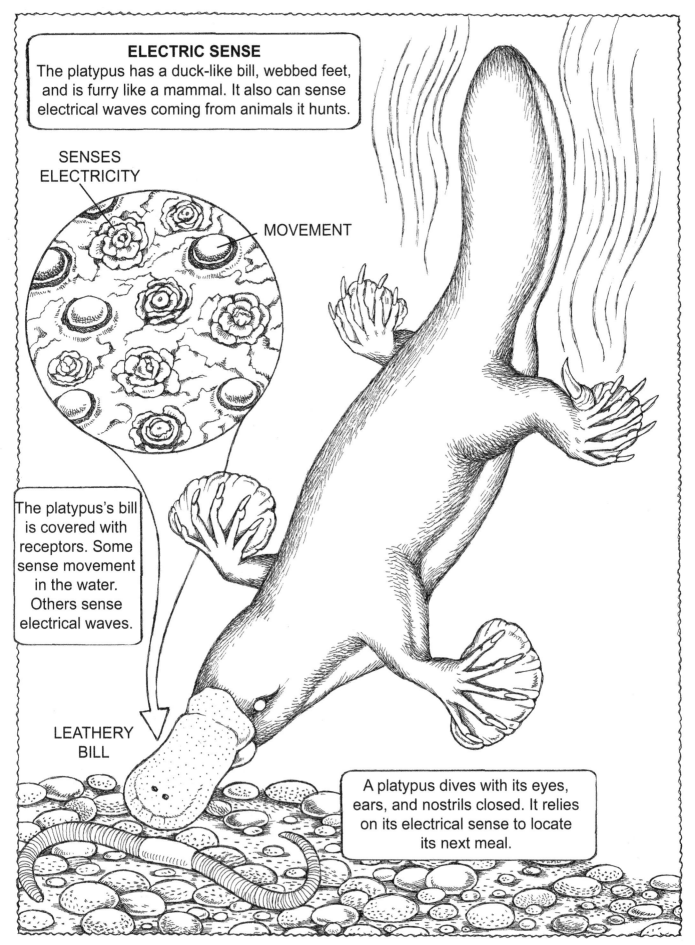

ELECTRIC SENSE
The platypus has a duck-like bill, webbed feet, and is furry like a mammal. It also can sense electrical waves coming from animals it hunts.

SENSES ELECTRICITY

MOVEMENT

The platypus's bill is covered with receptors. Some sense movement in the water. Others sense electrical waves.

LEATHERY BILL

A platypus dives with its eyes, ears, and nostrils closed. It relies on its electrical sense to locate its next meal.

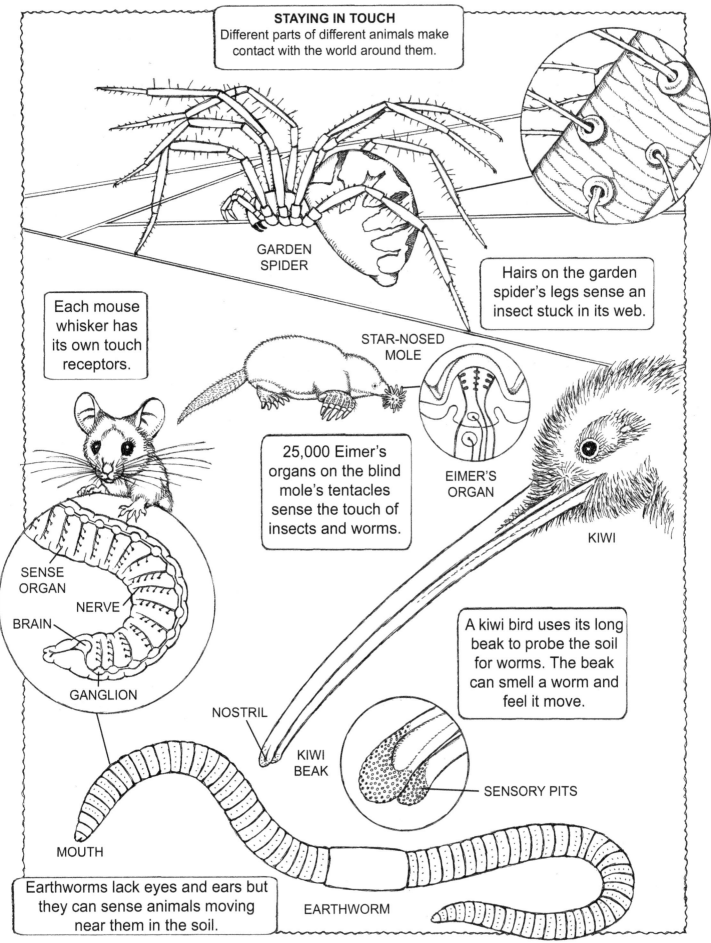

STAYING IN TOUCH
Different parts of different animals make contact with the world around them.

GARDEN SPIDER

Hairs on the garden spider's legs sense an insect stuck in its web.

Each mouse whisker has its own touch receptors.

STAR-NOSED MOLE

25,000 Eimer's organs on the blind mole's tentacles sense the touch of insects and worms.

EIMER'S ORGAN

KIWI

SENSE ORGAN

NERVE

BRAIN

GANGLION

A kiwi bird uses its long beak to probe the soil for worms. The beak can smell a worm and feel it move.

NOSTRIL

KIWI BEAK

SENSORY PITS

MOUTH

Earthworms lack eyes and ears but they can sense animals moving near them in the soil.

EARTHWORM

35

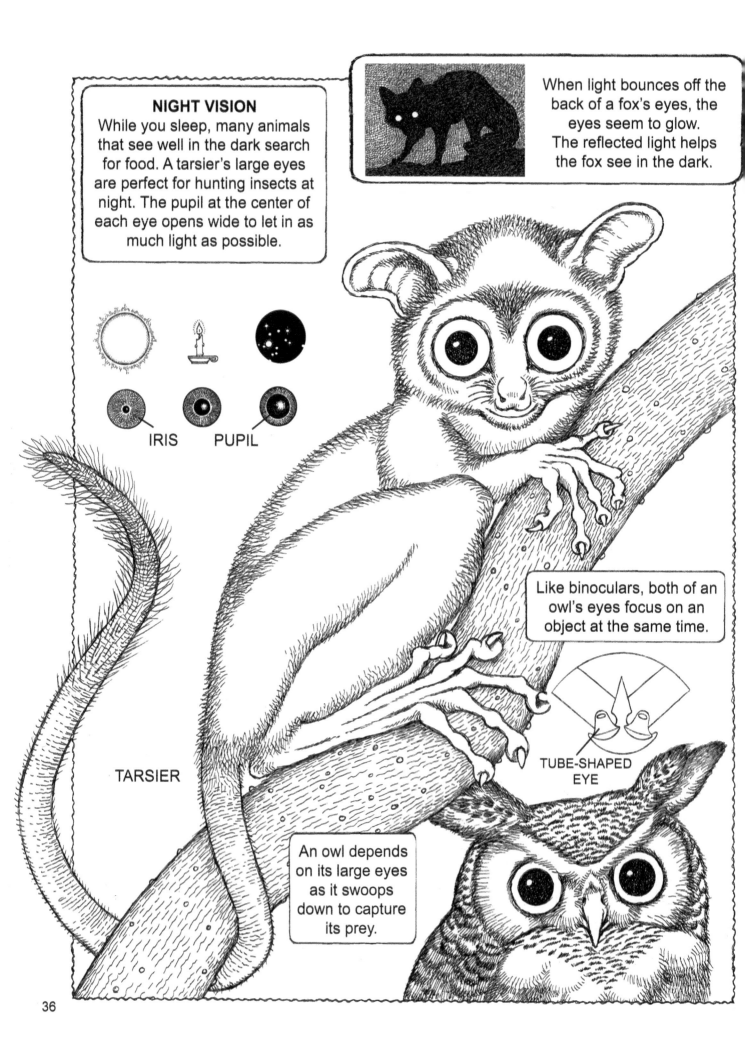

NIGHT VISION
While you sleep, many animals that see well in the dark search for food. A tarsier's large eyes are perfect for hunting insects at night. The pupil at the center of each eye opens wide to let in as much light as possible.

When light bounces off the back of a fox's eyes, the eyes seem to glow. The reflected light helps the fox see in the dark.

IRIS   PUPIL

TARSIER

Like binoculars, both of an owl's eyes focus on an object at the same time.

TUBE-SHAPED EYE

An owl depends on its large eyes as it swoops down to capture its prey.

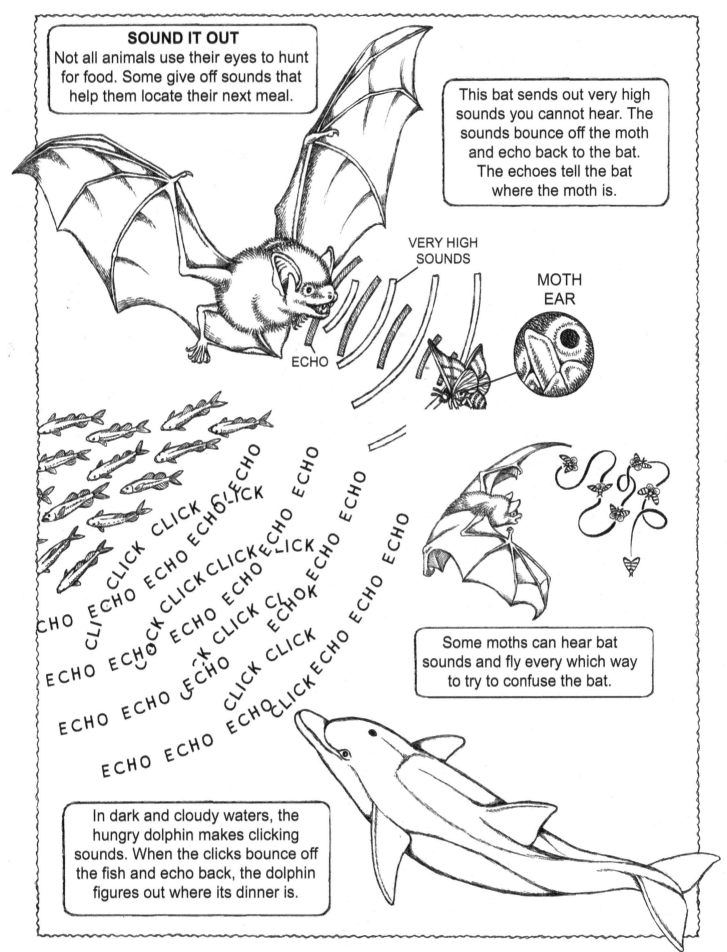

SOUND IT OUT
Not all animals use their eyes to hunt for food. Some give off sounds that help them locate their next meal.

This bat sends out very high sounds you cannot hear. The sounds bounce off the moth and echo back to the bat. The echoes tell the bat where the moth is.

VERY HIGH SOUNDS

MOTH EAR

ECHO

Some moths can hear bat sounds and fly every which way to try to confuse the bat.

In dark and cloudy waters, the hungry dolphin makes clicking sounds. When the clicks bounce off the fish and echo back, the dolphin figures out where its dinner is.

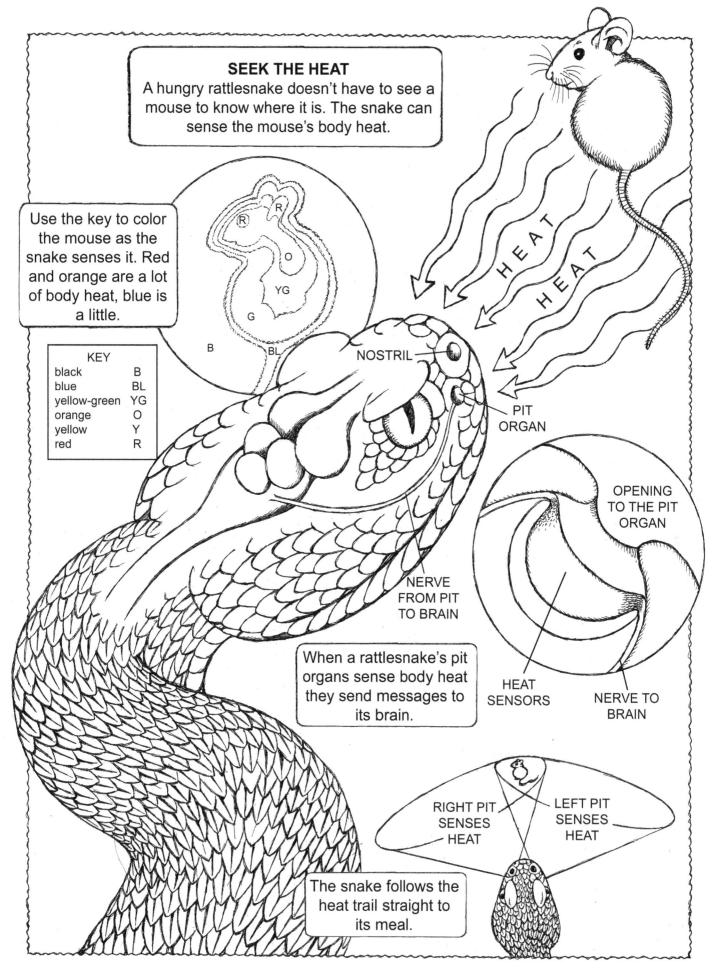

SEEK THE HEAT
A hungry rattlesnake doesn't have to see a mouse to know where it is. The snake can sense the mouse's body heat.

Use the key to color the mouse as the snake senses it. Red and orange are a lot of body heat, blue is a little.

KEY

black	B
blue	BL
yellow-green	YG
orange	O
yellow	Y
red	R

HEAT

HEAT

NOSTRIL

PIT ORGAN

OPENING TO THE PIT ORGAN

NERVE FROM PIT TO BRAIN

When a rattlesnake's pit organs sense body heat they send messages to its brain.

HEAT SENSORS

NERVE TO BRAIN

RIGHT PIT SENSES HEAT

LEFT PIT SENSES HEAT

The snake follows the heat trail straight to its meal.

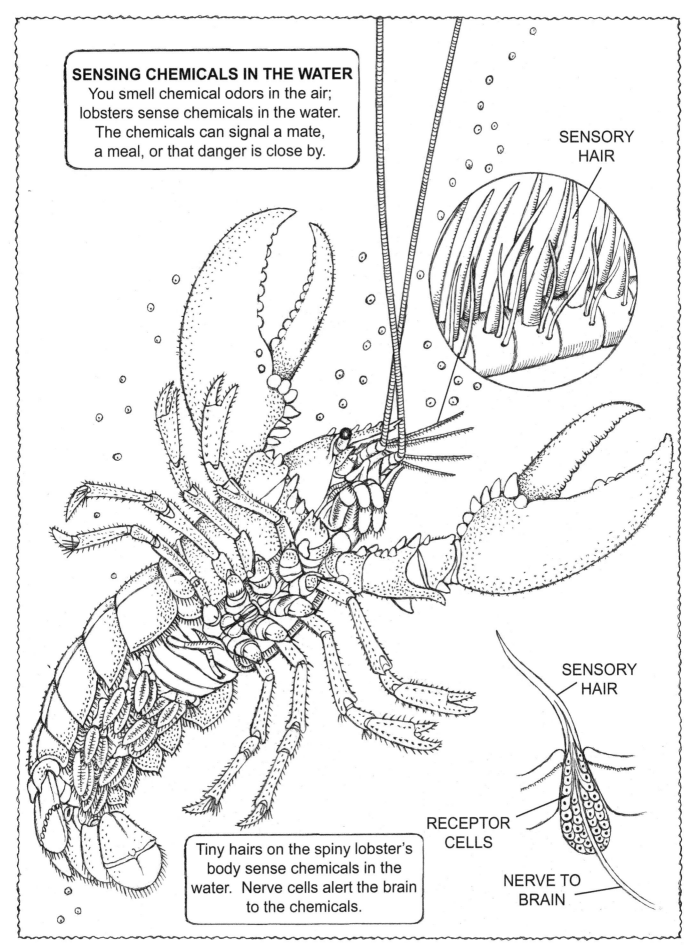

SENSING CHEMICALS IN THE WATER
You smell chemical odors in the air;
lobsters sense chemicals in the water.
The chemicals can signal a mate,
a meal, or that danger is close by.

SENSORY HAIR

SENSORY HAIR

RECEPTOR CELLS

NERVE TO BRAIN

Tiny hairs on the spiny lobster's
body sense chemicals in the
water. Nerve cells alert the brain
to the chemicals.

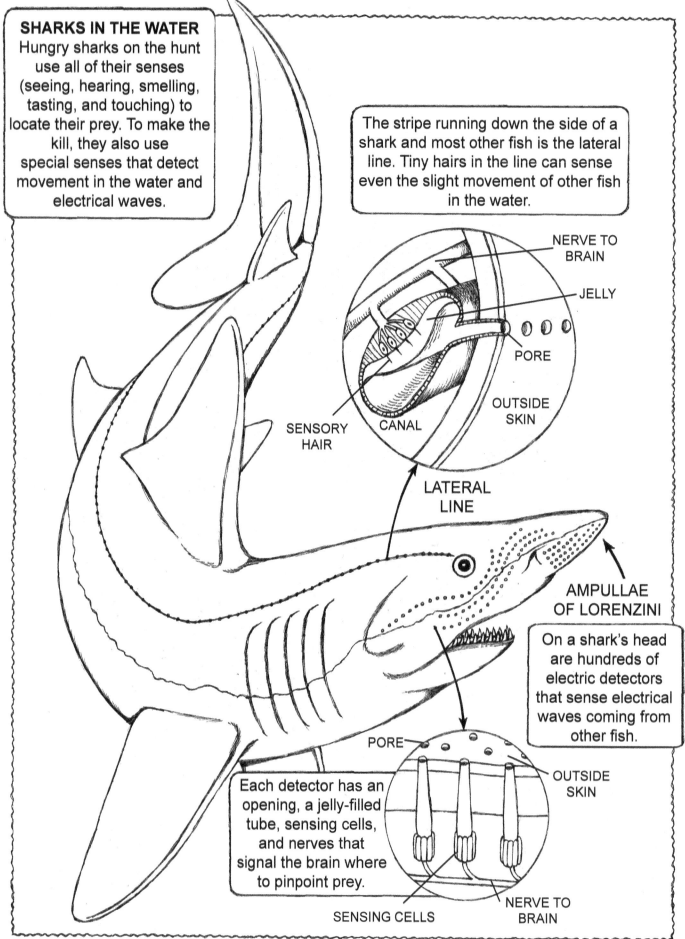

SHARKS IN THE WATER
Hungry sharks on the hunt use all of their senses (seeing, hearing, smelling, tasting, and touching) to locate their prey. To make the kill, they also use special senses that detect movement in the water and electrical waves.

The stripe running down the side of a shark and most other fish is the lateral line. Tiny hairs in the line can sense even the slight movement of other fish in the water.

NERVE TO BRAIN

JELLY

PORE

OUTSIDE SKIN

CANAL

SENSORY HAIR

LATERAL LINE

AMPULLAE OF LORENZINI

On a shark's head are hundreds of electric detectors that sense electrical waves coming from other fish.

PORE

OUTSIDE SKIN

Each detector has an opening, a jelly-filled tube, sensing cells, and nerves that signal the brain where to pinpoint prey.

SENSING CELLS

NERVE TO BRAIN

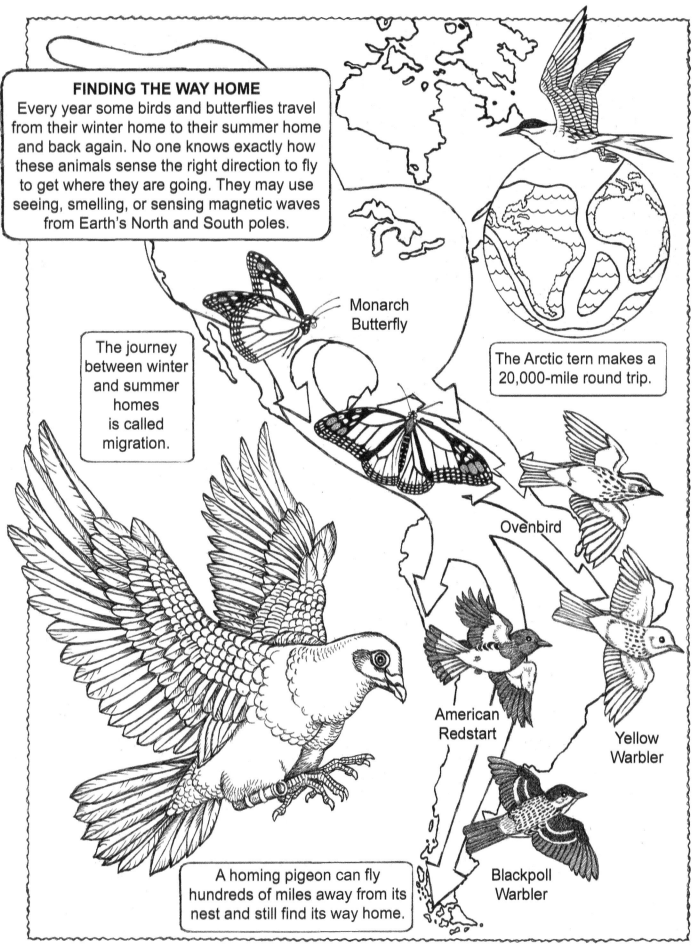

FINDING THE WAY HOME

Every year some birds and butterflies travel from their winter home to their summer home and back again. No one knows exactly how these animals sense the right direction to fly to get where they are going. They may use seeing, smelling, or sensing magnetic waves from Earth's North and South poles.

Monarch Butterfly

The Arctic tern makes a 20,000-mile round trip.

The journey between winter and summer homes is called migration.

Ovenbird

American Redstart

Yellow Warbler

Blackpoll Warbler

A homing pigeon can fly hundreds of miles away from its nest and still find its way home.

FOOLING THE SENSES
The shapes, colors, and patterns on an animal's exterior can fool the senses of other animals.

Can you find the two moth caterpillars on this twig? Predators can't either.

A white polar bear and a white fox can be difficult to spot on white snow.

When a leaf mimic butterfly lands on a branch, it seems to disappear. Two landed here. Where are they?

This isn't seaweed. It is a leafy sea dragon.

Three ways of fooling a predator are shown on these frogs. What do you think they are?

The Io moth and Calico butterfly are mimicking the same thing. Can you guess what?

RIGHT SIDE UP
Animals walk, run, jump, leap, swim, and fly. They depend on their sense of balance to safely get where they are going.

Like a tightrope walker, a squirrel can walk across a wire without falling. Its inner ear sends balance signals to its brain, and it uses its tail to help steady its body as it moves.

STATOCYST

COMB JELLY

Statocysts help balance a comb jelly in the water and help it stay right side up as it swims.

If a cat falls from a tree branch, it uses its sense of balance to tell which way is up and which is down. It turns its flexible body so that it lands safely on its feet.

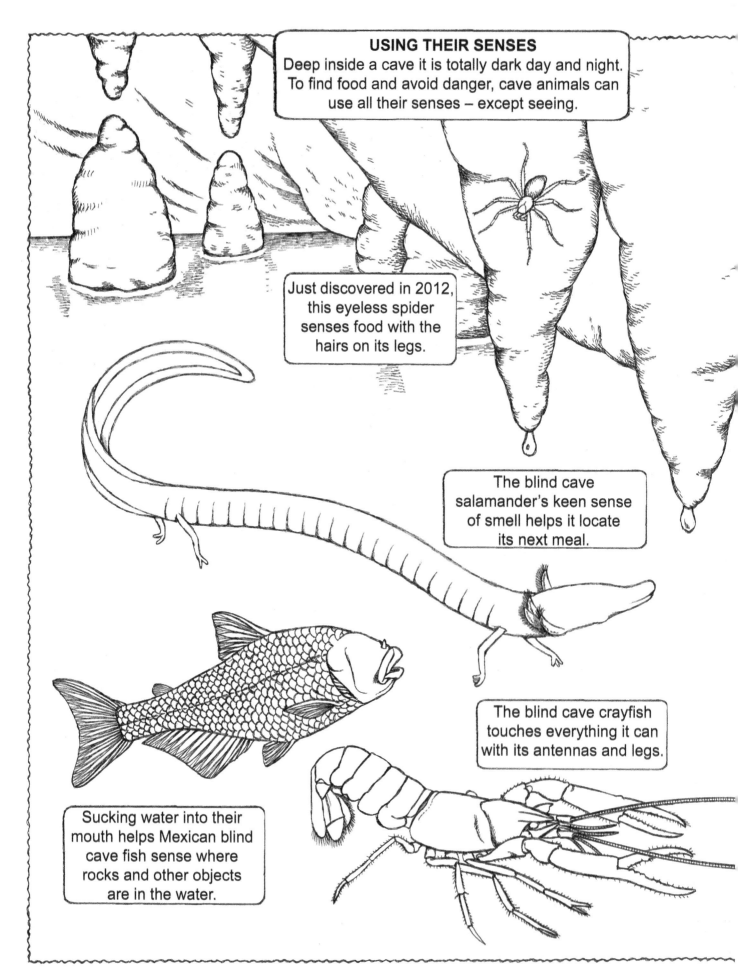

USING THEIR SENSES
Deep inside a cave it is totally dark day and night. To find food and avoid danger, cave animals can use all their senses – except seeing.

Just discovered in 2012, this eyeless spider senses food with the hairs on its legs.

The blind cave salamander's keen sense of smell helps it locate its next meal.

The blind cave crayfish touches everything it can with its antennas and legs.

Sucking water into their mouth helps Mexican blind cave fish sense where rocks and other objects are in the water.

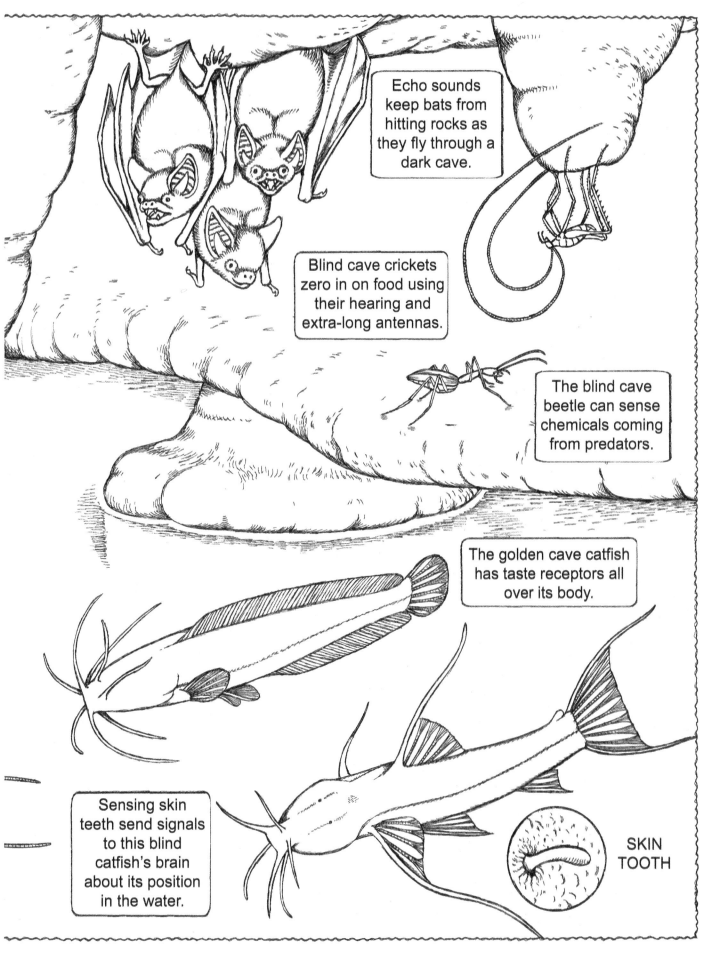

Echo sounds keep bats from hitting rocks as they fly through a dark cave.

Blind cave crickets zero in on food using their hearing and extra-long antennas.

The blind cave beetle can sense chemicals coming from predators.

The golden cave catfish has taste receptors all over its body.

Sensing skin teeth send signals to this blind catfish's brain about its position in the water.

SKIN TOOTH

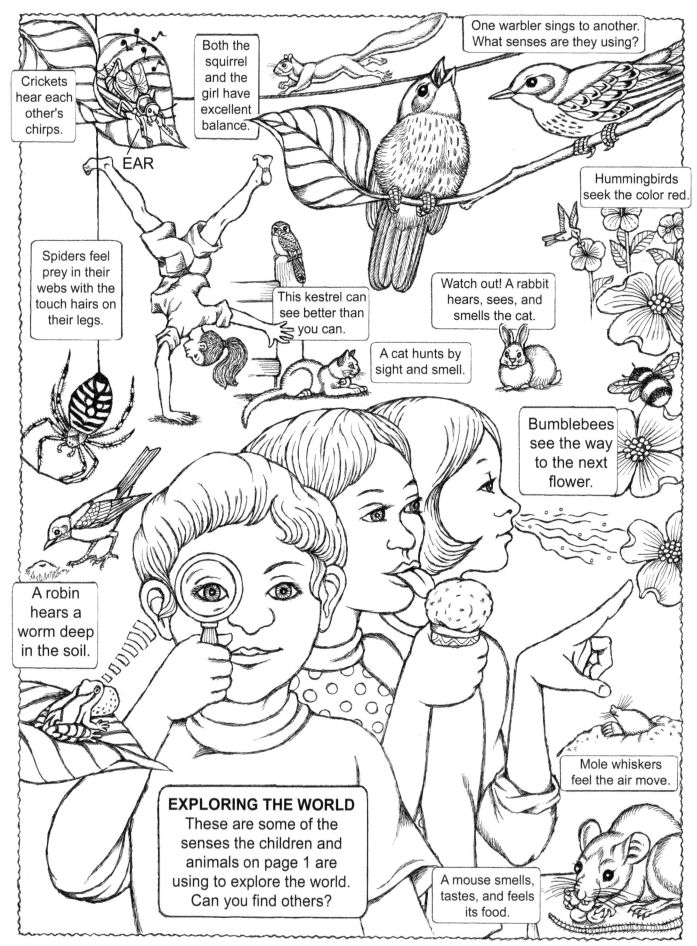

Crickets hear each other's chirps.

Both the squirrel and the girl have excellent balance.

One warbler sings to another. What senses are they using?

EAR

Hummingbirds seek the color red.

Spiders feel prey in their webs with the touch hairs on their legs.

This kestrel can see better than you can.

Watch out! A rabbit hears, sees, and smells the cat.

A cat hunts by sight and smell.

Bumblebees see the way to the next flower.

A robin hears a worm deep in the soil.

Mole whiskers feel the air move.

EXPLORING THE WORLD
These are some of the senses the children and animals on page 1 are using to explore the world. Can you find others?

A mouse smells, tastes, and feels its food.